DAVE COVINGTON

THE MEMOIRS OF

Sam

and

Chasity

To my mama, my ex-wife, and my stepsons for their encouragement throughout the years.

Contents

Chapter 1

The Beginning

Sam sat on the beach, reflecting on his life. Looking out onto the sunset, wondering why his life turned out the way that it did. What could he have done to change it? Maybe if he had changed before now, she would still be here.

The reflections of the sunset seem to reflect the life that he lived. The sun burns hot in the day then just slowly fades away during the night. Sam's life, like the sunset, has faded away. Let Sam backtrack so that you can understand where he comes from.

Sam was born with the name Sam Wilder. He was born in Colorado on September 1, 1970. He was born to a Native American mother who worked as a waitress at the local café. His father was in the US Navy at the time. His father made it through Vietnam, finished his four years of service, and was discharged from the US Navy when Sam was born.

Both his mother and father were very young, and he was their first child; he was not a love child though. His parents were married when he was conceived. His father had issues with drugs, alcohol, and controlling his emotions. A lot of this had to do with his upbringing and going to Vietnam. His mother had mental illness and was very emotional also. His parents did the best that they could with the experience that they had, or lack of experience I should say.

Sam's father and mother lasted only a couple of years in their marriage. Ever since then, Sam was raised as an only child by a single mother. She was great, though. She would play with him at the park, go to most of his sports games, and discipline him as needed. She did all this while working full-time at the little café in town. It was the only one in town but had the best food. Sam was only nine years old and in the 3rd grade, but he felt comfortable in the kitchen even at that young age. He helped in the kitchen as a dishwasher, prep-cook, and dishwasher. He would work for a few hours then go home to do homework if there was any and it wasn't a weekend. As a matter of fact this was his first job. Sam went to McClave Junior High and High school through his junior year. This was in the mid to late eighties.. It was a small school and a small town. The whole town was possibly four city blocks. Mostly made up of country kids. Outside of town was grass, countryside, crops, and farmers. Sam only had one true friend. His name was Robbie. Life in school at that time consistew d of school sports, riding four wheels, jumping in hay stacks, and of course barn dances and bonfires. Barn dances and bonfires would actually be considered Keggers. Students would get together at each other's houses to drink, listen to music, and talk about upcoming events. You could smell the hay and the alfalfa along with the liqueur. Most of the students including Sam chewed tobacco at the time. The school community had a lot of pride. Unfortunately, for Sam, outside of his one friend Robbie, he was a loner. He had several school fights. Sam had little fear of anything. He had his fair share of going to the principal's office. They were on a first name basis.

Sam went to school in a very small town, and he only had a four-day school week. The school and community had a lot of pride. Unfortunately, for him, he was a loner and a fighter. He was constantly getting into school fights and spending time with the principal. He quit playing football during his freshman year in high school. He continued to play baseball for all four years. He played third base and outfield.

Sam noticed that as the years started going by, his mother was not looking as good as she did before. She looked tired and run-down. He figured that it may have been all the years of working and that she was just tired.

* * * * *

Time had passed, and she told him she wanted to have a talk with him. "It is time for me to slow down," she said.

"Are you doing okay, Mama?" Sam asked her.

"I am going to be fine, honey. Don't worry about me," she said. "I have more to tell you," she continued. "I have arranged for you to go and live with your uncle John. I want you to finish school there. He has agreed to take you on," she stated with sadness on her face. You could tell that she was fighting back the tears.

"I don't want to go. I will not leave you alone. What is truly going on, Mama? Are you bad sick?" Sam replied with tears in his eyes. "I promise that I will do better in school, and I will not fight anymore. Please do not send me away," Sam begged her.

"I apologize, honey, but this is something that just must be done. Your uncle is a nice fellow with a wife and kids about your age. You will be okay, and you will have a good time," she said, trying to hold it together and not cry. That following weekend, Sam left Colorado, on his way to Arkansas.

When he arrived at the airport in Arkansas, Sam believed that his uncle John brought the whole family with him. There were several aunts, uncles, and cousins. They were dressed differently, looked different, and spoke differently than Sam was used to back home. "Welcome home to Arkansas," Sam's uncle, John, said as he gave Sam a hug that could have crushed a bear.

His Aunt Martha gave him kisses all over his face. He thought that it was going to turn his face red from all the lipstick. The cousins were all different sizes, ages, and colors. Sam knew about being a different color in the South because he was a Native American half-breed.

It wasn't long before it felt like the whole town knew that he was there. People were looking out their windows or staring from the broken streets. Uncle John and Aunt Martha were from Sam's father's side of the family. Even though his father was not around anymore, they still took him in as if he were still around.

When they arrived home, Sam got a chance to meet the rest of the family. Who knew that there would be more? These were the elders of the family that he did not have a chance to meet since his arrival into town. They were sitting with their drinks at the table, waiting for everyone else to come home. Grandma evidently loved to drink her vodka, while Grandpa loved his whiskey or bourbon.

The dinner spread looked amazing. There was fresh chicken that was killed and plucked that day and mashed potatoes and gravy (the potatoes were grown on their land). The fried okra, purple hull peas, collard, and mustard greens fresh from the garden. Let us not forget the Southern sweet tea for those of us that do not drink alcohol. This was a special meal that was made in Sam's honor but not far-off from a typical meal in a small country town.

Other than the chicken and the grease (to fry things like okra), he enjoyed the food since he was and has been a vegetarian for a long time now. After the supper meal was eaten, most of the adults retired to the living room, while a few of the aunts and the children, even the teenagers, helped clean up. Then it was time for a little relaxation, brushing his teeth, and going to bed after a long day.

* * * * *

The following day, Sam awoke to one of the elderly men poking him with his cane. "Time to wake up," he said in a softer voice. Sam asked him nicely to leave him alone. The elderly man continued to poke Sam with his cane and was now speaking in a louder voice. Sam asked him what time it was. He said that it was five o'clock in the morning. The elderly man then went on to explain that chores needed to get done before Sam went to school. His chores were to feed the chickens, collect the eggs, and feed the fish that were in the fishpond that was on the small farm. He did it begrudgingly and only after a cup of coffee. He normally doesn't drink coffee due to the caffeine, but this situation called for a cup of joe.

After his chores were done and breakfast was eaten, he prepared himself for the first day of hell. Sam rode in the back of the pickup truck down a dirt road to get to the little high school. There were only eighteen seniors in Sam's upcoming senior year. Of course, the boy-to- girl ratio was astronomical. It is no wonder why teenagers of different grades and ages dated each other.

Sam came from a small town in Colorado, but this was ridiculously small. As Sam walked the halls and went from class to class he noticed the stares, the whispering, and the talking behind his back. Comments related to him being, Native American, his braid, how he was different and did not belong at their school. He was shoulder checked in the halls more times than he could count. Then came the time that he was waiting for, he knew that it would happen eventually, he was challenged to an after school fight.

Sam imagined that he was talking about his long-braided hair. So he replied to him, "You are just jealous that even with my long hair, I am more of a man than you will ever be. In my cultural heritage, my hair is a symbol of strength, pride, and spirit," Sam explained to him in frustration. "I am sure that you have something in your hillbilly White culture that you take pride in, just as much as I do my long hair," Sam continued as he started to calm down a little.

The guy thought about it, smiled, then said that Sam was an alright guy. They then parted their separate ways and went to class.

Chapter 2

New School

Sam just happened to be one of those guys that did not back down from a challenge, and he never did. This poor sucker showed up to fight him after school, but he brought his friends with him. This also was nothing new for Sam, to be challenged by one person but then be jumped by a few others. "So, tough guy with a braid, are you ready for a bloody beating?" the one in the middle said. "You are nothing but a half-breed, and you don't belong here," he continued.

"So why don't you do something about it?" Sam simply said as he smiled back at him. They didn't care for his smile and started to attack him. It was the typical dirty boxing and wrestling that you see from most street fighters, especially from unskilled teenagers in Podunk towns like the one Sam happens to be in.

Sam was not one of these typical teenage fighters. He has been studying Tae Kwon Do since he was seven years old. He also had a slight bit of karate study in his teenagerhood. Sam's father, before he left Sam and his mother, told his mother that he wanted his son to study martial arts.

These guys did the best that they could, but the fight ended with them being battered and bruised. Sam sent a message to anyone else that wanted to challenge him. If someone did challenge him, then they would end up battered and bruised also. Sam didn't catch anyone's name, nor did he care to know. The only name that Sam wanted to know was the cute little blonde from English class. He didn't realize that she was at the fight and that he made the wrong impression on her.

* * * * *

The following day was not unfamiliar to Sam, it may have been a different state, city, and school, but the one thing that stayed consistent was that he did not back down from a fight. The other consistency would be him getting to know the principle on a personal basis. It was a good day and other than the Principal, of course, heard about the fight and called Sam into his office. He stated, "I cannot have kids fighting on the school grounds and leaving wrong impressions for the other students."

It was then that Sam replied, with a smile on his face, "I will not apologize for the fight. If it had not been for your students trying to jump the new kid in school, then I wouldn't have had to protect myself." "Do you find something funny about this, because I do not," the principal said in a stern voice. "I have seen your school records, young man." he continued in a stern voice.

"I will tell you this: you are going to have to learn to chill out a bit, otherwise you are going to make yourself sick," Sam said with a smile still on his face. "As far as the fighting is concerned, I will take on anyone dumb enough to fight me, and I will always protect myself. Can I go back to class now and try to learn something from your prestigious school?" Sam continued in a sarcastic voice.

"Get back to class and try to be good," the principal replied with a smirk.

Sam went on through the school day in a good mood, or as good as he could make it. All the students had heard about the fight that happened the previous day. Some of them were happy with him for taking on the bullies; others were not so happy. Sam's little blonde-haired girl would not even make eye contact with him in class or the hallways. They had never spoken to each other, but the chances of that happening just became slightly slimmer.

One of his cousins went to his locker to talk to him. "You know that little blonde-haired girl that you have been eyeing? Her name is Chasity Leann Jones. She comes from a rich family, at least for this area. She lives on a farm ranch outside of town. They have chickens, pigs, goats, cattle, and horses. She must wake up early before school and go home right after school to do her chores and studies. She rarely has time for anything else. Her father is an alcoholic and is abusive to her and her mother. Mostly verbal but can get overzealous in disciplining her and her mother," Sam's cousin said in a courteous manner. His cousin then continued, "She had passed by the fight after school yesterday and noticed that it was you. After she noticed it was you, she then associated you with her mean father. She had told her girlfriends that she liked you and wanted to get to know you, but this was prior to what she saw from you yesterday after school."

Sam then heard the bell ring, and it was time for class. Sam spent the rest of that day contemplating what he could do to change himself. All he was doing was hurting himself and his potential for the girl that he liked, even though they still had not spoken. He went home not as happy as when he had left this morning.

When he arrived home, Uncle John was on the porch sipping some lemonade, taking a break from his afternoon chores. He had seen the concerned look on Sam's face and asked how school had gone.

Sam was not usually one to talk to other people about his troubles, but Uncle John had a kind heart and was not judgmental. So Sam spilled the beans, as they say, and told his uncle all about the fight, the principal, and the girl.

His uncle's response was loving and kind but very simple. He said, "Son, you must always protect yourself against all people. I am not opposed to fighting, but I am opposed to starting a fight or not walking away when you can. As far as the principal goes, he is an idiot. He does not know how to run a school any more than a donkey knows how to be a show horse. When it comes to the girl, I know her family. They have been a staple in this town for many generations. Alcohol and abuse run through the generations. I feel very bad for the family and people that must be around them. If you can help anyone, you need to help her. The only way that you are going to be able to deal with your problems and issues is to make a change in yourself. After you change your perspective, then you can help others. Do you understand?"

Sam replied, "It sounds like I am going to have to change myself from the inside out if I am going to make it in this world. I know I acted like I was proud of who I was, but the truth is that I do not like myself very much."

Sam's Uncle John then said, with a smile, "I know all about your parents and where you come from. It has not been easy for you, but you have a lot of spirit in you. And you will do well in life," as he went back to work.

It was after that talk that Sam knew what he had to do. He had to go back to his native roots. He had to find a calm spirit through his culture. He had to be conscious of the hawk flying in father sky as well as all the animals that roam mother earth. He asked permission to put up a teepee and a sweat lodge on his aunt and uncle's land. He stated that he wanted to build a sweat lodge and Teepee to help center himself and reconnect with his spirit. His Uncle just smiled and told Sam that his mother used to do the same thing. So Sam found that fascinating, that he could be like his mother and build a sweat lodge.

It took him about a week to figure out how to build the sweat lodge and teepee. He looked at old books that he got from the library. He was a modern- time Native American and did not have the previous knowledge of his mother's generational past.

After a week, he had his sweat lodge up and the pit built for the heat. The following day, after he had everything built, he was able to go in and try to connect to his spirit. He went in, sat cross-legged, closed his eyes, and breathed in the steam from the pit. After a while, he started to sweat and hallucinate. He saw spirits in the sky that were looking down on him like guardians. He felt their spirit enter him as if they were entering his soul. He knew that he was going to be all right because he knew that the spirits were going to watch over him in his life.

When he talks about spirits, he means ancestors of Native Americans that have passed from the earth but still watch over their people from the sky. Upon leaving the lodge, and after wiping away his heartfelt tears, he felt renewed and ready to tackle the world.

Chapter 3

Sam Meets Chasity

Upon leaving the sweat lodge, Sam's new family, as usual, had a feast—no occasion, just a family meal. It happened right on time too because Sam was a Starvin' Marvin.

Sam spent the rest of the evening playing checkers with his uncle and listening to country music. He liked to listen to some of the older country, such as Hank Williams, Earnest Tubb, Roy Clark, Patsy Cline, Loretta Lynn, Hank Snow, and others. Sam had no clue who these people were prior to arriving in Arkansas.

Sam liked to listen to Guns N' Roses, Poison, Arrowsmith, Snoop Dogg, Dr. Dre, etc. A total difference in styles. Sam did come to like some country music, though—not so much of the oldies but goodies. He came to like Travis Tritt, George Strait, Garth Brooks, Randy Travis, and a few others. He became quite eclectic when it came to most music. Most every night he would spend playing games with the family, whether it was checkers, cards, dice, or board games. The exclusion to this was sometimes watching Disney movies with the younger cousins or watching sports with the grown folk.

When Sam arrived back at school, he was a new person. Not brand- new like a shiny penny, but more like a polished bell that you can still see some rust on. He arrived at school in his normal chipper mood. For those who know Sam, this is a funny thing, because his normal chipper mood is quite different from what other people would consider chipper. "Hey, Sam, how are you doing today?" Sam's cousin and his friends said as they met him by his locker.

"Today is the day, boys. Today is the day," Sam replied with a big smile on my face.

"What are you up to now, cousin?"

"I hope nothing stupid, or that is going to get you into trouble," they continued.

Sam could not keep the grin off his face. "I am going to talk to her today," Sam replied.

"Talk to her who?" they all said in chorus.

"I am going to talk with my little blonde angel from English class," Sam responded.

"I told you before that she does not like you because she sees you as violent," Sam's cousin replied.

Sam responded with his chest out and his head held high. "She may not like me now, but she will soon enough," Sam stated as the bell rang to return to class.

While entering class, he noticed her in the front row on the left side, closest to the window. She was a daydreamer like him and loved to look out the window. He was always wondering what was going on in her head and what she was thinking about while she was looking out the window. As for Sam, he just enjoyed watching her. She loved to look out the window. She would daydream and get lost in the blue sky with fluffy clouds. She would daydream, not of being a princess or finding Prince Charming. She would daydream about a normal life when she could be loved for who she is and not because of her parents' stature. She would dream about when she would be able to leave town. Nowhere fancy just out of Arkansas and find true love with someone that she could love and he would love her back. She kept these as private thoughts and dreams.

"Okay, class, this week, we are going to study poetry," the teacher said with a grin. Most of the class growled and grumbled, but not Sam. He loved poetry because it was so interesting in its many different forms. For an abstract thinker like himself, this was right up his alley. "Today's assignment is to write a haiku," Mrs. Patty said with a smile.

Jimmy, who sat in the back row and was just as much of a smart aleck as Sam, replied, "Why do we have to write a haiku? We live in America, not Hawaii," he stated with a smirk on his face.

Mrs. Patty took it in stride and replied to him, "Hawaii is part of America. Haiku is a traditional Japanese art form of poetry, and now you know two things that you can keep in that thick skull of yours." Mrs. Patty smirked back.

Maybe this could be the opportunity to show not just the blonde girl, but everyone else more of my sensitive side.

We were told that we could write the poem on anything that we wanted as long as we followed the traditional five-seven-five syllable format. This was one assignment that he got to right away and did not put off until later. Of course, he had ulterior motives, though. So he wrote a couple of different haiku poems for his young lady that he felt smitten with.

Haiku Number 1

Dreams come true for me.

Your spirit shines through the dark skies.

I have found my way.

Haiku Number 2

You are an angel.

The sea shines through your blue eyes

My heart beats for you

Sam was anxious to turn the assignment in so that it could be graded, and then he could give it to her. He thought that it was pretty good, if he did say so himself.

The teacher was impressed with his poetry skills as well as his writing skills. Sam was never good with proper grammar, conjunctions, punctuation, and the like; but most of the rest of English, Sam was pretty good at. English was his favorite subject in school, with math being his second favorite. Sam was never much for the rest of it. He did very well at lunch and recess, though.

Anyway, back to the task at hand, and that was to give the poems to the girl that he was smitten with. He figured this would be a good icebreaker for her and for himself. He caught her after class as she was walking with her friends going to the water fountain. "I know that you do not know me very well, and I may have given you the wrong impression of myself the other day after school. I also know that people have been talking to you about me, which would also leave you with the wrong impression of me. I just wanted to tell you that I am not who you think I am, and I wanted to give you these poems to show you my softer side," Sam said, scared as hell that she was going to reject him. "I would like to get to know you better and have you get to know me better. To tell you the truth, I like you a lot. There is no one else in this school that I would rather be with," Sam said with a half grin.

"I will take a look at these and get back to you later," she replied with a half grin. He noticed, as she walked farther down the hallway, she turned and gave him a little smile. That little smile meant the world to him and gave him hope that the world was going to be all right. Sam finished the school day and went home with joy in his heart.

When he arrived home, it seemed that the word had already gotten out about what he did in school. His cousins made it home prior to him arriving home and had to tell everybody right away. The smiles and hugs were given to him right away by the whole family. "So what is it like to be the great poet and wooer of women?" his uncle said while snickering.

"You just leave the boy alone and let him enjoy this moment in his young life," his aunt replied, while hitting his uncle across the back of his head. "I recall a time when you were romantic and would write me poems. Now all you do is drink, belch, and scratch your butt.

How could any woman resist you?" his aunt continued with a half grin.

His cousins also had comments to say about the issue. "So, stud muffin, how is it going with your dream girl? I think that you might actually have a chance with her if you don't mess it up by being yourself," his oldest cousin commented.

It was such a wonderful day Sam wasn't going to let anyone's comments or snickers affect him in a negative way. He went to bed that night, feeling that he just might have a chance at happiness with a girl.

Chapter 4

Sam Dates Chasity

When Sam went to school the next day, everyone in his class already knew about his feelings toward Chasity. When you go to a small school, it does not take long for people to know and be up in someone else's business.

To Sam's surprise, it was Chasity who had spilled the beans about his feelings toward her. To top that off, she responded by also telling people about her feelings toward Sam. From that point, it was inevitable, the feelings that they shared as one heartbeat.

They are officially dating now. He gave her his class ring to wear, and she wore it with such pride. They had several dates out by the lake. The lake was not completely clear, it was a little murky. The grass and trees were still green but with a tint of brown since it was the fall. You could hear the breeze whistle through the trees. It was the perfect spot for a picnic and swimming. Picking the right time was very important since Arkansas rains more than Colorado did. Sam remembered their first date. They had packed a picnic lunch that turned into a picnic dinner. They continued to swim and talk about everything and nothing.

Sam wanted to know all about her, and Chasity wanted to know all about him. Sam didn't lie during their conversation, but he left some things out. Things were going so well that he didn't want to mess things up. He could see in her body language and facial expressions that she was holding back also. Like they both had deep dark secrets that were too early in the relationship to talk about.

As night came they watched the sun slowly come down from the sky forming a beautiful sunset. Once the sunset was at the horizon it produced an amazing picturesque glow on the lake. Shortly after the stars came out and shone upon the lake. As they were finishing their picnic supper under the stars, a gentle rain began to fall. At that moment Sam could not keep his eyes off of Chasity. The way that she glowed in the moonlight, Watching the rain come down her cheeks, rolling over her pink moist lips, then continuing to drip off her chin. He didn't think the moon, stars, or rain did anything for his looks; but Chasity could not have looked any better. He knew that they were going to be together from that moment forward.

They had several dates after that, but nothing would match that first one. Little did Sam know that her parents didn't approve of them. They knew that Sam and Chasity were dating, but they did not approve of the different social classes mixing. Sam remembered their first kiss. It happened when they went and parked at the top of the road, where you could look down and see the town lights. "This is so romantic. Thank you for bringing me up here," Chasity said with a smile.

"I know that taking you to picnics at the lake, having movie nights, and doing some of the other things that we have done are less expensive. Maybe they are not up to your standards, but I can only do the best I can," Sam replied with some sadness.

"Where is that coming from, Sam? I appreciate everything that you have done for me. Our social classes are different, but our hearts are not. I do not care about what anybody says. You are my boyfriend, and nothing can change this fact," she said with that grin of hers.

"I know that you deserve better, but I appreciate the fact that you care about me and the things that we have done together. I have fallen in love with you, Chasity," Sam said with a smile.

"I love you too, and I don't want to be with anyone else, Sam," she replied with a smile. Then it happened.

She leaned toward him with her eyes closed ready to be kissed. Sam pictured that night at the lake how beautiful she was with her moist lips. She had that same beauty and perfect lips this evening. He leaned in and their lips met for the first time. They held their lips together and embraced for what seemed like eternity. for that moment in time , all the stars, planets, and universe were aligned in their world. Even though they were both seniors in high school, it was both their first kiss.

They lost track of time, and they arrived home after curfew. For Sam, whatever punishment given would be worth it. Sam just did not want to get her in trouble. He had a feeling her parents did not approve of him and Chasity. As he was told before, he was out of her league. She came from a rich family, and he did not. This did not change the fact that they had fallen in love with each other.

It was now the time in their lives that they were full of life, love, and innocence. They were young and had their whole lives ahead of them. They felt the way that most young lovers do, that love will go on forever and never change. This was the case for Sam and Chasity. They were starstruck lovers that walked the moon and never wanted to come back to earth.

Senior prom was just around the corner, and the butterflies were starting to flutter around Sam's stomach. He was excited to go to prom with the most beautiful girl in school. He knew that she felt the same way about him.

Everybody else was left out of the equation. Sam and Chasity did not care about what their families, friends, classmates, or townsfolk thought about them going together. They knew who they were, where they came from, and where they stood in society. Nothing stopped their true feelings for each other.

It was prom night, and Sam was in a suit that his father left behind when he left the family. His dying mother from Colorado made sure that the suit made it to Arkansas in time for the prom. This was the same suit that his father wore when he married his mother, as the story was told. Sam felt proud to wear the suit and he felt good about himself.

Sam was preparing for prom. He had showered, brushed his teeth, braided his hair, and put his suit on. He was about to walk out the door when his aunt hollered at him to come to the living room. "Other than the suit, your mama sent you something else," she said.

"Well, what is it?" Sam said in an excited voice.

"I told your mama about you and Chasity. She gave me her diamond earrings for you to give to Chasity," she said with tears in her eyes and hugged Sam.

"I am so overwhelmed, Auntie, with the suit, earrings, being accepted, and being in love," Sam said while crying and hugging his aunt back.

"You be on your way, boy, and you love each other as no one has ever loved before," Sam's aunt said with a smile.

"I shall, Auntie, no doubt about it," Sam replied with a smile.

When he arrived to pick up Chasity, he was met with the familiar look from her parents. That type of look of disgust. The look that says, *Our daughter is too good for that half-breed.* Sam was used to it by this point, so it did not bother him anymore. He just smiled, waved, and greeted them with as much respect as he could muster.

Then Chasity came out in a white dress with blue trim. She had curled her hair, and it fell softly upon her shoulders. She had makeup on but not too much. Just enough to accent her face. Thoughts raced through Sam's head. She is the most beautiful girl that I have ever seen. She truly is an angel, not just her beauty, but her soul. She makes me feel like I can fly and do the impossible when I am with her. I am excited to be with her at the most important school event for Senior Year. " So are you ready to go? " Sam said, with a grin.

"You bet I am," Chasity replied with a smile. "You have her back before one -o-clock, young man" her father hollered at Sam. Sam just smiled and opened the door for Chasity,his prom date.

"I will take that into consideration," Sam replied with a smirk.

After arriving at the school, and before going in, Sam pulled the earrings box out of his pocket. "I have a surprise for you, Chasity," Sam said.

"What did you do now, Sam?" Chasity replied. She opened the box with a look of awe on her face.

"These were the real diamond earrings that my mama gave to me to give to you," Sam said with tears in his eyes. Sam and Chasity hugged and kissed each other in the car prior to going into the senior prom. They spent the rest of the evening dancing, smiling, laughing, and looking into each other's eyes. All as if the outside world never existed.

They left prom early because he had supper reservations in the next town. He took her to the nicest place that he could find, for that part of Arkansas. He ordered a Steak, shrimp, and baked potato meal, that they split into two plates. He made sure that the table had a candle and a yellow carnation, Yellow Carnations was Chasity's favorite flower. After the meal he took her home. He walked her to the door and gave her a kiss goodbye. This night will be forever burned into Sam and Chasity's mind.

* * * * *

It was now time for graduation. *Where did the time go?* Sam thought to himself. *What am I going to do with my life, and how can I do it but keep a relationship with Chasity?* Chasity was not only beautiful and smart but she was also their valedictorian. They had a graduating class of eighteen kids getting ready to graduate, but most were not ready for the world. This was not the case for him and Chasity. They did not know what they were going to do, but they knew that they were ready to tackle the world.

Chapter 5

Family Troubles

After every graduation, there are always graduation parties; small-town Arkansas was no different.

Sam invited Chasity over for the graduation dinner at Uncle John and Aunt Martha's house. The spread was the usual feast. At some point during the dinner, Chasity started to feel a knot in her stomach and throat. She started to get a little dizzy. She had become anxious and overwhelmed. Chasity had been around large crowds before, but nothing as loud and proud as Sam's family.

Chasity grew up in a more sheltered home. Her father was a bit overbearing and socially drank a lot. He would often have his moods, where he would come home and smack Chasity and her mom around if they did not do things correctly, according to his tastes and desires. She was not able to leave the home, except for school and social functions in the society that they lived in.

Chasity started dating Sam without her parents' permission by sneaking out of the house. Then Chasity's mom caught her sneaking out of the house one day and found out about Sam. It was a secret between mother and daughter until her father beat it out of her mother. He did not like the idea of mixing races, even if it was only dating. Chasity's father allowed her to date Sam if he got his needs met by Chasity's mother.

"Sam, I must leave and go get some air. You can stay with your family if you would like, but I must leave now," Chasity said with sadness in her eyes.

"What is wrong, Chasity? If it is my family, I know that they can be overwhelming, but they love you to death," Sam replied, looking a bit confused. "We can skip supper and meet up with some friends if you would like. Or even better, we can go to our favorite spot in town and just be together," Sam said, trying to make sense of what was going on.

"Give me a minute, and I will meet you back inside. I am a little bit peckish, and I do love your family. After supper, we are going to have to have a talk, though," Chasity said while still holding her head down and not making eye contact. Sam did not know what to think about the situation, so he quietly walked back into the house.

"Is that sweet child all right?" many members at the supper table asked as Sam returned.

"She will be all right. She just needs to take a moment," Sam said while trying to keep his emotions in check.

Chasity showed back up and walked to the supper table shortly after Sam did. "Are you all right, girl?" Sam's aunt said with concern.

"Yes mam, I am all right, and I want to thank you for your concern. You truly do make a girl feel loved in this household. But everything looks good, and I am hungry. So can we eat now?" Chasity replied, starting to perk up.

"You bet we can. Come on, everybody, have a seat so that we can bless the food," Sam's aunt replied with a smile. Sam's aunt had the funniest smile because she would smile with no teeth. The meal went well, and Chasity had a chance to meet Sam's crazy-but-loving family. The only one that was not there was Sam's mother. She was still in Colorado.

After supper, Chasity and Sam said their goodbyes and headed to the car. Sam's family could tell that Chasity was a troubled young girl. She was very sociable and polite but troubled. Sam opened the door for her, like he has always done. Sam learned the art of being a gentleman to ladies from his mother. "Sam, I am not in the mood for any party tonight. Can we go out to the river and talk?" Chasity asked, still not looking Sam in the eyes.

Sam drove her to their favorite picnic spot to have a talk. He could tell that this was going to be a serious talk and not like any other talk that they have had. They arrived at the spot right as the sun was going down. It was the most beautiful thing in the world. To see the hues of colors in the sky as the stars started to come out. Sam looked up into the sky and saw the first star. He then quoted to Chasity, "Star light, star bright. First star I see tonight. Wish I may, wish I might. Grant me this wish I wish tonight." This quote sent Chasity into tears. The exact opposite effect that Sam was hoping for. "Is my voice really that bad?" Sam said, trying to brighten Chasity's spirits.

"No, Sam, it is not, but I need you to listen because I need to have a serious talk with you. I don't want you to say anything until after I am done talking. Can we agree on that?" she said in a very serious voice.

Sam then started thinking, *What the heck did I do wrong now?* In his past, anytime someone wanted to have a serious talk with him, it was because he did or said something wrong.

"Sam, I and my mother have been abused by my father for as long as I can remember. He has been a mean drunk and is very verbally and physically abusive. Instead of protecting me, my mother lets it happen for fear of her getting beat harder, for trying to stop it. Therefore, I wear long sleeves and dress fancy to school, and in society, to hide the bruises. Therefore, I would not let you see me in my swimsuit or underclothes outside of the water when we swim. I would love to wear regular clothes, but I cannot due to the bruises and my shame. Also, my parents are trying to keep up appearances. I am a part of their high-class appearance. Therefore, I have to put on this act that I am a socialite and act properly around other people, because if I do not, then there are consequences.

"I know that my mother loves me, but she just doesn't know how to help me. So when she saw that I was with a down-to-earth boy like yourself, she became very excited for me. I have never felt true love before I met you and your family. Therefore, I had a hard time with your family at suppertime. I am not used to a true loving family or to have someone like you that truly loves me," Chasity said while sobbing into her hands.

"Can I say something now?" Sam tried to eke out the words.

"No, you may not. I have more to tell you," Chasity replied. Chasity continued, "I will be moving as far away from here as I possibly can. I chose to go to Berkeley in California for college. I love you more than anything in the world, and I have enjoyed our whirlwind romance for our senior year. But I must go. I must get away from the abuse. I cannot watch my mother be abused anymore, and I cannot follow you or wait for you."

"Can I say something now?" Sam replied, trying to get a word in.

"No, you may not. I told you I have more to get off my chest," Chasity replied while still crying. "I am going to California early this summer before my fall semester starts. I know that you are going into the Navy to start your career. That said, we will only have a month left to see each other. I appreciate all that that you have done for me and the whirlwind senior year romance that we shared. I will always love you, and I feel sad that we must part ways," Chasity said, sobbing in her hands and unable to complete her thoughts.

"Chasity, I have to tell you my story also since you have revealed yours. My father was in the Navy during Vietnam. The war messed with his mental status, and he was mentally ill after serving his four years. Instead of regular medication, he took to drugs, alcohol, and womanizing. When he was home and sober, he was a good father and husband. When he was not, he was horrible. He was also verbally and physically abusive to my mother. He never was abusive to me. He loved me with all his heart, but he was young and did not know how to be a father or husband. My parents separated when I was young, and I was raised by my mother the rest of the time.

"A few years ago, my mother found out that he had committed suicide. One of his many kids tracked us down and told my mother, who eventually told me. Evidently, the failed marriages and the failed relationships with his children, along with the drug and alcohol abuse, was too much for him to take. This is the reason why the blue suit that I wore at prom was so important. This is also why the Navy is so important to me. It has been a tradition to be in the Navy through my father's lineage. Then to top everything off, my mother is dying of acute myeloid leukemia. She was in stage 4 when they found it, and it had already metastasized. My auntie took me aside shortly after I arrived and told me the whole story. Now I know why my mother sent me here to Arkansas. So that she can die at home without me watching her through the process and finding her dead.

"I am all alone in this world, and your love means more to me than anything. I do have somewhat of a solution, though. My plan is to go to boot camp and A School training to be a hospital corpsman in San Diego. I can come and see you during my liberty and my time off from school. How does that sound?" Sam asked with tears in his eyes, trying to keep the relationship going and his hopes up.

"I am sorry to hear about your mother and father. That must be tough on you. I want you to know that I am here for you whenever you need me. I do not know how our future is going to turn out, but because of our upbringing, we are strong-willed and have a more realistic view of the world than most other kids our age. That said, I do not know how realistic it is going to be to try to continue this relationship once I go to college and you go into the Navy. I say, let us enjoy what we have at this moment in time," Chasity said in a realistic voice, not sobbing anymore.

Leave it to a woman to be realistic about life plans, Sam thought to himself. "I do not like it, honestly, but I do have to agree that right here and now in our relationship is what we need to think about," Sam replied, not crying anymore.

Both Sam and Chasity were about cried out by the end of the evening. They spent the rest of the night just holding each other in a warm embrace and kissing each other under the stars as if it was their last time.

A month's time had passed, and it was time for Sam and Chasity to part and go their separate ways. "I love you, Princess. Call me from that fancy college of yours and stay in contact," Sam said with a grin but was really trying to choke back the tears.

"I will, Cabana Boy. You have fun playing sailor in the Navy. I might be around for you to contact me," Chasity said jokingly with tears in her eyes. The terms Princess and Cabana Boy were created out of the affection they had for each other. Sam watched her drive away, and then he returned to his Uncle John and Aunt Martha's house.

Chapter 6

Mama's Funeral

Sam had only Seen Chasity a few times since his Mama's funeral. He saw her when she would come home from school on her breaks and holidays.

His mama got the funeral that she wanted. The service was by invitation only, with a few family members and friends. The urn was navy blue with gold trim, Navy Colors. The music was Cristy Lane's "One Day at a Time," Elvis Presley's "His Hand in Mine," "Mansion Over the Hilltop," "Amazing Grace," "Peace in the Valley," and "I'll Remember You." These were some of his mama's favorite Christian songs. She always said that no one can sing better Christian songs than Elvis can. She was enamored by him.

Her flowers were a variety of colors and sizes of daisies. Sam did not speak at the funeral. Sam was more of the quiet type and wanted to keep things to myself. There were only a few people there, family and friends, that Sam wanted to share this experience with.

After the funeral, Sam took the urn home and placed it on his bedroom dresser. He would eventually come back to getting around to spreading the ashes. Sam's mama wanted to be scattered among the many casinos and beaches that they visited across the United States. That will eventually happen, but now it was time for the wake. This was also by invitation only.

Since Sam's mama passed in late spring and toward the beginning of summer, Sam held the wake in his mama's and his backyard. Sam loved to cook, so he created a crawdad boil to go along with the beer and alcohol. He made it traditional by boiling the crawdads, baby potatoes, and corn on the cob in Cajun seasonings. Once the food was cooked, he lined the tables with newspaper, drained the water, and poured the food onto the newspapers. The wake lasted through late into the night with listening to 50's and 60's rock and roll, people laughing about old stories of mama, eating, and drinking.

Sam went back into the house early. He looked at the urn and talked to her as if she was still there. He told her about the love that he had for Chasity. How he had plans of joining the Navy. He found out through friends that she had seen his graduation picture right before she passed. He reminisced in his mind the life that he and his mother shared. Now it was time for him to be an adult. They both came from abusive homes, they both ran away from home, they were both taken advantage of by men at a young age, they both suffered miscarriages, and they were both ambitious in life. In Chasity's scenario, she would often run away after her father came home drunk and abusive. She was in the social service system a few times, with Child Protective Services being involved; but the judge kept recommending that she return to her rightful parents.

She had a proper aunt and uncle that wanted to take her into their home, but the judge wouldn't allow it. One of the times that she ran away, she met a boy that promised her the world and would take her away from everything. This was not the case. He had his way with her and left her in the streets. She had no place to go but to return home.

Upon returning home, her father found out and asked her to have an abortion. He did not want a child out of wedlock to spoil their status in society. "This baby has done nothing wrong. It is not the baby's fault how he or she came about. I am keeping the baby so that I can have somebody to love me!" Chasity yelled back at her father.

This angered him, and he kicked her in the stomach. Chasity fell to the ground where her father continued to kick her, causing her to miscarry. These things came out over time after Sam's mama's passing. Sam felt horrible finding out these things about what the girl that he still loves went through.

He had not seen Chasity but a handful of times since Graduation. Years had passed with him taking care of his mothers wishes by spreading her ashes and his personal need to travel. He wanted to be able to tie up loose ends and grow up a little bit ,prior to joining the Navy. Chasity was almost done with her sophomore year, by the time Sam had joined the Navy. He continued to have hope and faith for their relationship. The affectionate, caring, loving, relationship that they had once shared. It felt like Chasity had moved on. The communication between them had started to fade. The visits were far between. They truly were growing up and going their separate ways. But Sam had to find out where she was. Sam spread his mama's ashes in San Diego, California; Redondo Beach, California; San Francisco, California; Rhonert Park, California; Las Vegas, Nevada; New Orleans, Louisiana; Shreveport, Louisiana; Biloxi, Mississippi; Cripple Creek, Colorado; Old Orchard Beach, Maine; Bangor, Maine; and Hawaii. These were some of the casinos and beaches that they visited among their travels. There were more places that they visited but these were the main ones, and he ran out of ashes.

He took time at each place to enjoy the memory of his mama. He knew that she would be pleased wherever she was. He knew that she was in no more pain and that she was laughing and having a great time once again.

Sam also took some time to do some traveling of his own outside the USA. He took an extra six months to go to India, Thailand, Costa Rica, Panama, and Ireland. These were just places that looked beautiful to him, so he took the time to go. He went to all these places on the little bit of money that he had saved. He also had the money from his mama's bank account since he was made her power of attorney and executor of her will. The will stated that he would receive everything that she had since he was her only child.

He was growing into a much better person and a nice young man. Not the ornery cuss that he had been in school. Well, it was time to be the man that he wanted to be and join the Navy. He would finally get the chance to be in California with Chasity, if she wasn't already with somebody else.

Sam joined the Navy like he said he would not only because he wanted to but because he wanted to fulfill his father's lineage and tradition of being a sailor. Boot camp was harder than he thought, with the physical training (PT), the swimming, the learning of technical terms of items in the Navy, and the Navy ships, learning the general orders, staying up late for guard duty, and waking up early at 0500 (5:00 am.). The recruits got to sleep in on weekends until sometimes 0630 (6:30 am.).

Option of church or being given an assignment to do in barracks was on Sundays. Sam always chose church not because he was religious but because he didn't want any extra assignments.

Mail call would come twice a week. Packages from home only once a week. A lot of marching and a lot of running. Sam missed out on the gas chamber due to having to go to the dentist and having all four of his wisdom teeth taken out. The gas chamber is where the recruits enter the chamber with their gas mask. When given the signal, they take their masks off and sing the ABCs.

Among other things, Sam learned a lot of different marching and running cadences. Sam always wondered what the relativity of marching and running as a group was to the military. Upon completing boot camp, he found out it was for learning to work as a group, morale, and comradery. Sam's company earned the right to call themselves Ironman since everyone in his company passed their final physical training (PT) test. Sam entered boot camp a relatively big guy at 205 pounds. Eight weeks later, he was 172 pounds. He felt as healthy as a racehorse.

Sam couldn't wait for the liberty whistle to be blown at graduation. As soon as he was released by the company commander, he headed straight to Berkeley to see his girl. Some of his fellow mates went home to see their family, while most went out celebrating; but Sam went out to Berkeley, only to find out that she wasn't there. The girls at her dorm stated that they did not know where she was. She had left earlier in the week and told them she had some serious business to take care of. Sam had a funny feeling in his stomach that he knew where she was going.

Chapter 7

A Murder in Arkansas

Chasity was on her way back home. It seems that she had got word that her mother had died due to blunt force trauma at the hands of her father.

Her father was in jail, awaiting trial for murder in the second degree. They could not call it murder in the first degree because it was not premeditated. Chasity was subpoenaed by the court to testify against her father. In most courts, a person is not allowed to testify against another family member. This was not most cases.

Sam had a feeling that she had gone back to Arkansas. He found out about the court case and wanted to be there for her, in her time of need. This was not the ideal situation to reconnect, but he still loved her and wanted to be there for her. He took his two weeks' liberty from boot camp, and prior to going to A School, to go and support Chasity. He went straight to her friend Emma Lou's House where she was staying.

When he arrived, Chasity was shocked to see him. It had been over a year since they had seen each other. She noticed Sam right away and went running into his arms. Crying on his shoulder, she said, "I knew that this was going to happen at some point. I just did not know when." Sam just held her close and whispered in her ear, "I will always be here for you no matter how far apart we are. You just need to tell the truth no matter what and keep no more secrets." Sam continued while still holding her tight.

They went to court together, along with what seemed to be the rest of the town. This was the most important event this town has experienced for as long as anyone could remember.

The courtroom was a standing-room only. And the crowd covered much of the space outside the courtroom and courthouse. It was a short trial due to the testimonies for the prosecution and the lack of testimonies for the defendant. It seems that this was one time that Chasity's father could not buy his way out of trouble.

The defense lawyer tried to rattle Chasity's cage by telling her about all the trouble that she had caused to her father. All the running away, getting pregnant, and the embarrassment she was to her father. The defense attorney also spoke on how Chasity's mother was never there for her father. She would always run away from her duties as a proper wife. These things, along with the stress of his job, caused him to often lose touch with reality, and he did not know what he was doing.

Chasity was angry and shaking at these accusations about what she and her mother had done. Moreover, that what was done caused her father to lose touch with reality and abuse them. Then to say that he was not in reality when he beat her mother, causing her to die from the injuries that were sustained. Chasity cleared her soul about her father and what he had done to her and her mother, without any fear of what society thought of her and her family. Once she had finished, there was barely a dry eye in the courtroom.

At the sentencing, which was one week later, the judge showed no sympathy and gave Chasity's father thirty years, which is the maximum sentence that he could give for a second-degree murder in Arkansas. Chasity had hoped never to see her father again in any situation, especially one like this.

As she walked out of the courtroom, she looked at him one last time. She did not have anything but distain for the man who killed her mother. She was bombarded by the people in town wanting to hug and comfort her. Sam helped her push through the crowd so that they could get into the car and get outside town, away from everyone, to have a little peace. "How did you know where to find me? How did you know that I needed you the most?" Chasity said from the passenger seat.

"The girls at your dorm said that you took off and they hadn't seen you in a while. They said that you had some serious business to take care of," Sam replied while driving Chasity out of town. "Plus, you forget my auntie has ears, and she knows almost everything that goes on in town. So when I couldn't find you, I called my aunt to see if she might have any news for me. As soon as I heard, I got a plane ticket from San Diego and came home to Arkansas to be with you," Sam continued with deep concern for Chasity in his heart.

"That is so sweet of you to do that. I thought that after these past couple of years with only a few visits, that you would have moved on" Chasity said with tears rolling down her cheeks. They just stared at and embraced each other for a long while.

"Like I said before, there is nothing that can stop me from getting to you. There ain't no mountain high enough, ain't no valley low enough, ain't no river wide enough," Sam started singing. "Besides, I told you I will always be here for you no matter what. My mama always taught me to keep my promises. So I always will keep my promises," Sam said with a smile. He wanted to reassure Chasity of his intentions with her. He still did not know if she was seeing someone else at school, but he knew that he would always be her first and last best friend.

Sam and Chasity went out to the lake where they had their first date. The lake still had its charm, but not like it did in their Senior year. It may have been because they have seen and been to other places. It may be the impact of their current situation. Nevertheless that is still their place. "I am extremely sorry that you lost your mother. Even worse, the way that you lost your mother. It is always hard to lose someone, but to lose someone from a tragedy is the worst way. You sometimes do not have the opportunity to say goodbye to them. I honestly do not know if you did or not, Chasity. I don't even know the last time that you saw her before the murder. I just know that I did not get to say goodbye to my mother before she passed away" Sam said , in a quiet but concerned voice.

"You're right. It is hard to come home to your mother dead at the hands of your father. The last time that I saw her was also the last time that I saw you, when I came home for the holidays. That was over a year ago. We talked on the phone regularly. I could tell by her voice that something was wrong, but I did not want to come home any more than I had to. I had just started a new life with new friends and a new location. I had been seeing a psychiatrist and therapist for my past trauma. I was doing good in my studies and living as good of a life as I could. I even had a nightlife with my friends. Now I feel guilty because I should have been able to protect my mother somehow, but instead I stayed away. And now she is dead. What am I supposed to do now? How do I move on from something like this? Tell me, Sam. Tell me, Sam!" she screamed, crying and punching Sam's chest.

"One day at a time. I know that it sounds cliché and simple, but it worked for me. Learn to love yourself and not blame yourself for anything. That is the hardest thing to do," Sam said with a tear rolling down his cheek and holding Chasity.

They spent the rest of the evening talking and holding each other. They did not know where their relationship was going, but they were going to be friends forever. The two weeks of leave were over, and Sam had to leave Chasity once again to go back to A School to become a Navy corpsman. Chasity also would be leaving soon to go back to school. Chasity and Sam engaged in a long embrace and kiss at the airport prior to Sam leaving for San Diego.

Chapter 8

Sam in Navy School

All that Sam could think about on his way back to San Diego was Chasity and her situation.

How was she going to be able to handle the situation? What effect would it have on her psyche? Would she be able to go back to school? How long would it be before he would be able to see her again? These questions, among others, plagued his mind. He loved Chasity with all his heart and soul, and it hurt him to see her hurt. All that being said, he would have to put some of that on the back burner and concentrate on his schooling.

Going to corpsman school was the biggest challenge that he would embark on. Sam Wilder was a street-smart person. He knew how to do things to survive in life, but he was not very book smart. He was really going to have to be on the ball and concentrate if he was going to pass this course.

It would then advance to burn care, drawing blood, putting in stitches, placing IV's in the vein, attaching IV bags and piggy backs, delivering a baby among other things with labor and delivery, These were the main things learned as a Corpsman, but certainly not everything.

Sam's favorite part of the training was putting in the clinical hours at the Balboa Naval Hospital. His favorite floors to work on were pediatrics, labor and delivery (L&D), and medical/surgical. He liked to work and learn hands on as compared to sitting in the classroom. Sam would often take on extra clinical hours because he loved what he was learning and doing.

One time, by choice, Sam stayed up for forty-eight hours straight between school and doing extra clinical hours at the hospital. His shipmates made sure he was good and asleep when he returned back to the barracks, and then they took him and his whole bed into the shower. They took a picture with several of them standing around him with his bed in the shower. They took several poses. They then returned his bed to the proper position in the barracks.

When he awoke, they told him what they had done. They also told him that they would give him the picture at graduation. Sam didn't believe them, but anything is possible among a bunch of young eighteen- to twenty-something-year-old sailors. For many of them, it was their first time away from home or at least their hometown. This was also Sam Wilder's first time away, other than moving to Arkansas from Colorado.

The structure of the school was that everyone went to school in the morning. They would then have a lunch break then return to school in the afternoon. After school was over if you were not assigned to a duty or had your clinical rotation, then the evening was yours to do what you wanted. There was no school on the weekends, but there were still duty assignments and clinical rotations.

Every corpsman had to spend a certain number of hours in the hospital on different floors. They also had to carry a certain grade- point average to pass hospital corpsman school. Sam Wilder was fairly sheltered when he was with his mother. Then he was also sheltered in Arkansas with his Arkansas family. So Sam spread his wings a bit with other sailors his same age. The two places that Sam liked to go to when he had the chance were the beaches and Tijuana (or TJ, as it was referred to). Sam had never been to the beach or outside the continental US. Sam had a good time and did get into mischief with his shipmates, but he was very well in control in most situations.

* * * * *

Chasity had not gone back to school yet. In light of her current situation she thought it would be a good idea to go back to therapy. So she sought a therapist and Psychiatrist in Arkansas. She has always displayed these certain behaviors, but she was never allowed to seek therapy for her problems while growing up. It just would not have been proper in her parents' social circle. She did keep several journals and wrote several books of dark poems.

She had sought therapy before for her past trauma and her dark feelings. It wasn't until her father killed her mother, that she realized how lost she really was and how much therapy she really needed. She was put on medication to keep her calm without being depressed. She and her therapist worked on regressive memories, as well as taking into consideration the murder. The therapist wanted her to start from childhood trauma and work her way through adult trauma. There was a lot of work to be done. She stayed at a friend's house in the next town over. This was a friend that she had grown up with but, due to circumstances, was not allowed to see very often. Her friend's name was Emma Lou, and she worked at Fred's, the local grocery store. Emma Lou stated, " I know that you cannot go back to the house and you are not ready to go back to school. You can continue to stay with me if you would like. I can get you a job at Fred's with me if you would like."

"I appreciate your offer, but I can't think straight enough right now to work a job or concentrate on school. I will however take you up on letting me stay at your house longer, though" Chasity said with appreciation of her friend Emma Lou.

This would allow Chasity not to have to suffer the stigma of living in the same town, where all the bad things happened to her. Chasity spent time healing from old and new wounds in her mind. She had a great place to do this with her friend Emma Lou. Chasity continued to take her medication and go to her Therapy appointments. Her stories and thoughts that she was writing in her journal were not as dark as before. She got to the point where she was having fun with her friend and even making new friends.

The longer that time went by, the better that she started to feel about herself. It had been about four months of intensive therapy, and Chasity was ready to go back to school. During the last four months, she and Sam had been in contact with each other over the phone. They stayed on the phone as long as they could and had long conversations about everything that had been currently going on. Neither one of them saw the need to talk about the past unless Chasity brought it up.

Sam had learned over the years that there were certain things that were not a topic of discussion due to hurt feelings. Sam would never want to cause Chasity any pain. Sam, of course, talked about how things were going in hospital corpsman school and where he was thinking about being stationed after he graduates. Chasity talked about how she was feeling better and where she might want to restart her schooling to become a registered nurse.

The time had come, and Sam Wilder was about to accomplish graduating from his A School in the Navy. As his name was announced, for a brief moment, he looked out into the crowd for his mama. She had always been to every event and graduation that he was involved in. Tears rolled down his cheek when he thought about her not being there for this graduation or any other future events. That being said, when his name was called, he noticed that Chasity had flown in to support him. Now he had tears of happiness once he saw her smiling at him when he walked across the stage.

Sam chose to go to Pensacola Naval Hospital as his next duty station. Sam wanted to check out the beaches in Florida. Chasity was not sure where she was going to land, but one thing for sure was that Sam and Chasity would always be one phone call away.

Chapter 9

Sam's New Duty Station

From San Diego, Sam could have taken another leave prior to arriving at his duty station in Pensacola, Florida, but he decided not to take his leave.

He was excited to go to the beaches of Florida and start work at the Pensacola Naval Hospital. The sleeping quarters were set up behind the hospital with two bunk beds, a bathroom, and a mini fridge in each room. There were four rooms per apartment. The common area was in the middle of the rooms. It has a table and chairs, two couches, a microwave, and a television.

As soon as Sam and his buddies arrived, they rented a car from the Airport. Then they went straight to the beach, jumped in, and played, as if they were still kids. After a nice swim, he went to grab a bite to eat with some of the other corpsman that flew with him from San Diego. On his way back to his apartment, he called Chasity to tell her how beautiful Florida was, especially the beach. "I am so excited to be here, Chasity, and my other shipmates seem to be happy also. I can't wait to really get to know these guys. One of my roommates is from Arkansas also. His name is Robert Chancellor. He just goes by Chancellor. He is just a big ol' country boy. He is almost twice the size of me," Sam said with a big smile on his face.

He would have kept going, but Chasity cut him off. "I know that you are excited, but I have some good news to tell you. I have decided to move to Florida to be next to you, support you, and get a fresh start for myself," she said in a happy tone of voice.

Sam's voice changed almost instantly. "You said that you are coming down to Florida to support me and get a fresh start for yourself. I am super excited that you are coming, but when you said, 'Get a fresh start for yourself,' am I included in this fresh start? Is it a fresh start for us or just you? I am just asking so that I can understand where you stand on our relationship," Sam said happily but somewhat concerned.

"As I told you before, Sam Wilder, I love you and will always love you. As far as a relationship, we will just have to play it out slowly," Chasity said in a discerned voice.

Sam thought to himself, *How much slower can the relationship get?* In his eyes, it was moving slower than a snail after eating a full meal. On the other hand, what she was offering could turn out to be a great experience for both. He was hoping that just as she wanted to support him in the Navy, he could support her by encouraging her to go back to nursing school.

She flew to Pensacola Florida, a week after the phone conversation. He met her at baggage claim. She was looking older and a bit worn down, but she was still his angel.

" So how are you doing this fine evening, my princess? Looking fine as ever from my viewpoint," Sam said with his cheesy grin.

" Not too bad, Cabana Boy, you are looking kind of sexy yourself. I have to tell you that this humidity is going to take some time to get used to. My hair is all frizzy" she replied with a huge smile.

He then took her into his arms and embraced her as they kissed. They kissed as if it was their first kiss.

Sam said " There is this great little cafe that I found that I would love to take you to, if you would like"

"Of course I will, I guess I can trust your taste in food", she said with a giggle." I found it on my first day here. It is not fancy, but it is charming and eloquent . Just like you, Mrs. Chasity Leann Jones." Sam tried to impress her with his words. He has been trying to impress her ever since he met her in high school English class. He continues to try to impress her even to this day.

"Well, Mr. Sam Wilder, I do have to say that I am impressed with your speaking skills. They have improved over the years along with your looks," Chasity replied with a smirk.

"Well let's get going, shall we?" Sam opened the door like a proper gentleman. Then they headed to the little cafe on the beach. They talked about several different subjects, just trying to do some catching up. They talk quite often on the phone when they are apart, but that is not the same as talking live and in-person. They tried to keep things positive in their conversation and not talk about the past.

The date went clear into the night. When they left the restaurant they could see the sunset glowing off of the beach. Sam's mind was on Chasity, but for a moment, as they were watching the sunset, he started humming the tune, "When the sun goes down over the water, everything gets hotter. When the sun goes down, what is a man/child supposed to do though when his mind starts to wander?"

They finished off the evening by stopping to get ice cream along the way. He was still a proper gentleman and walked her to her apartment. The apartment was not quite set up as of yet, but the bed was set up for her. The landlord also left her some furniture to start with. She would figure out the rest later. Sam went back to his apartment, looking forward to the next day so that he could spend more time with Chasity.

That next morning was shopping for small appliances and other essentials needed for her apartment. They went all over the place, looking for specific items that Chasity wanted to have in her apartment. In this sense, guys are much different from girls, especially a guy like Sam. Sam could get away with no-name brands and live with only the very bare essentials. Women tend to want things more decorative and things that they feel that they have to have to make them comfortable. So what Sam thought might take a few hours of shopping took all day, apart from stopping to eat and drink at Sam's request. Had he not suggested, then she could have shopped all day just on the nutrition that was left from last night's supper.

The evening had finally come, and it was time to go back to her apartment to start the set up. Sam had no say in anything all day; he was just the honey-do guy. He was the mule that loaded and unloaded the car. When it came to the apartment, he only did what he was told to do by picking up and placing things here or there. Sam and Chasity talked briefly prior to saying their goodbyes with a kiss and a hug.

Sam returned to his apartment to get ready for muster the following day. Muster, in civilian talk, is to get ready for inspection. Every shift must muster before they start their shift. Every corpsman must have his or her body, hair, and uniform, among other things, look presentable to other staff and patients. This was also the time to explain if a corpsman was sick or not. If they were sick, then it was up to the person in charge to either send them home or work depending on how sick they were.

After muster then they would have a meeting describing the patients' diagnosis and treatment for the day. After this is done, then assignments are given out, and the workday starts. A corpsman would work under the officer in charge. Sam finally got to start work as a hospital corpsman. He officially got to do the things that he had studied and did his rotations back in A-School. Sam and Chasity were both starting out fresh and getting away from the horror that they called their past—or so they thought.

Chapter 10

Sam Marries Chasity

After they were both settled in, they officially rekindled their relationship and started dating again.

Often when the other corpsman were off duty, they would go to the dance clubs, bars, or strip clubs. This was not the case for Sam Wilder because he had made a promise to Chasity that he would stay on the straight and narrow if they were going to be together. They would often go to the beach, out to dinner, the movies, or other activities that did not involve drinking.

Sam had been socking away money a little bit at a time in order to one day buy Chasity an engagement ring if the time was ever right. Well, now it seems that the time was right. He knew exactly what she had wanted unless she changed her mind. He remembered going to the jewelry store with her back home in Arkansas. She liked the classic white-gold setting with four prongs and the cushion-cut diamond. She fell in love with it, but neither one of them had money at the time, especially enough money for a diamond ring.

Now times have changed, and Sam was ready to propose to that little girl from English class. He arranged to have a bonfire on the beach, and right at sunset he was going to pop the question. Most of his shipmates disagreed with Sam's decision except for Robert Chancellor. Who knew that the big guy would be so sensitive to love issues? Looking back Sam should have known that Chancellor was sensitive despite his size. They would often watch Disney movies together. Their favorite movies were *The Princess Bride*, *Lady and the Tramp*, and *Blood Sport*.

Sam met Chasity at Destin Beach, in a spot that was designated for bonfires. His plan was going well. They ate a nice supper, and when the sunset started, Sam reached into his pocket, got down on one knee, and proposed to Chasity.

"Chasity Leann Jones, I have loved you ever since I had laid eyes on you. We have been through many trials in our lives, and through the support of each other, we are where we are today. Our friendship will last forever, and so will my love for you. I would like to take the next step and ask you to be my wife," Sam said with a nervous and cracking voice.

"I told you before, Sam Wilder, that I will let you know when I am ready for a more serious relationship with you. I have asked you several times in the past not to push the issue," Chasity replied in a serious voice and a serious look on her face. She then smiled and started giggling. "Of course, I will be your wife. You have always been there for me through every aspect of my life. I love you with all my heart, and I would love to marry my best friend." They then sealed the proposal with a kiss while listening to the waves come to the beach.

It had been about a year and a half since the proposal, and they decided to get married at Sam's next duty station. In the meanwhile, Sam left the base life to live with Chasity in her apartment. Sam's next duty station was Bethesda Naval Hospital in Maryland. Bethesda Naval Hospital was in a suburb of Washington, D.C. Sam would still have his normal patients as far as the sailors, but he would also take care of people that were in the government.

Sam wanted to take his career a little more seriously, so that is why he chose Bethesda as his next duty station. Sam's aunt and uncle came out for the wedding. Sam also had a few cousins show up. Chasity had a few friends that she made in college show up for the wedding as well as her brides maid Emma Lou from back home in Arkansas. Chasity had a few friends that she had made in college fly out for the wedding. Emma Lou from Arkansas flew out and was her Bridesmaid. They chose a fall wedding due to the color changes of the leaves and how beautiful the East Coast looks in fall.

Sam wore his Navy dress blues, and Chasity wore a beautiful white dress that fanned out on the bottom. The dress had beads that were sewn into the neckline and chest. The dress had a small train attached, and her wedding veil came down to the middle of her back. The veil was also adorned with beads.

Neither Sam nor Chasity had a bachelor or bachelorette party. They had chosen long before the wedding that they would not have a bachelor or bachelorette party. They just wanted to have a combined dinner party with their friends.

The wedding was not formal. There were no rehearsal dinners, no cake tastings, no church ceremony, and no gift registry, and it was done with only a few friends and family. The ceremony took place in one of the buildings that was rented in town. The ceremony was performed by one of the naval chaplains. The day of the wedding Sam and Chasity were both nervous.

Chancellor was Sam's best man. Chancellor flew in from Pensacola, Florida, to be Sam's best man. He made sure Sam looked impeccable. He continued to talk with Sam to keep his nerves down and keep him ready for the future. Emma Lou, who was Chasity's maid of honor, did the same for her. She helped get her ready by calming her nerves, getting her dressed, and doing her makeup and her hair. No salon was involved. This wedding was done on a shoestring budget.

Sam, Chancellor, and Emma Lou took their places by the Chaplain and waited for the music. The music played, and Chasity started walking down the pathway with another shipmate of Sam's; his name was Henry. Henry was one of the corpsman that Sam made friends with at Bethesda.

As they approached, the chaplain asked, "Who gives this woman away?"

Henry responded with a resounding, "I do, sir." The Chaplain quoted the normal wedding verses from the bible. Sam and Chasity had written their own vows. " Chasity, I have loved you ever since the time that I laid on you in High School. I know that we have had our troubles, but I like trouble. I want a lifetime of getting in trouble with you. If you would have me as your husband?" Sam said with a smirk. " Sam, I just might be more trouble than you can handle. I have fallen head over heels for you, my troublemaker. So would you have me as your wife? Chasity was smiling from ear to ear. Now it was the time that they had waited for since they were teenagers." Do you, Sam Wilder, Take Chasity Leann Jones, to be your wife in sickness and in health, for richer or poorer,to be her constant companion, till death do you part?" Heck ya I do. Sam replied with a huge grin.

The chaplain continued, "Do you, Chasity Leann Jones, take Sam Wilder to be your husband in sickness and in health, for richer or poorer, to be his constant companion, till death do you part?"

"You bet your boots," Chasity replied with an even bigger grin.

"Then by the power invested in me by the US Navy and the state of Maryland, I now pronounce you husband and wife. You may kiss the bride," the chaplain stated with a smirk on his face. The kiss was one for the ages. It was a kiss that would have long-lasting memories.

Sam and Chasity did not go on a honeymoon for a couple of reasons. They wanted to save some money for living expenses, and it was not time for Sam to take another leave, as of yet. So instead, Sam took Chasity to her favorite restaurant and spared no expense. They had steak and seafood.

The seafood in Bethesda was as fresh as it could be. From the restaurant, he took her out dancing. Sam very much disliked dancing, but he knew that Chasity did; so he took her to one of the local clubs that played a variety of music. That night, Sam had a pep in his step and got onto the dance floor and danced. He mostly did line dancing and slow dancing with his new wife.

Afterward, they went to their apartment off the naval complex. They had to wait for married housing to open since they were now married. This was the best night of both of their lives, and they were making plans for the future. Maybe even having a child and starting a family of their own. Who knows what lies in the future?

Chapter 11

Chasity Gets Pregnant

The beautiful wedding was over, and so was their night out.

The next morning, while lying in bed, holding each other, Sam leaned over and whispered, "So, Mrs. Wilder, how does it feel like to be a properly married woman?" Sam said with that big ol' cheesy grin that he can sometimes get.

"Well, Mr. Wilder, it is like this. I have been betrothed to you for many moons now. I am proud that you made me a proper wife. I am even prouder to have you as my husband," Chasity replied with a smile.

"Now you are just trying to make me blush. I do not blush easy, but with the fancy way that you speak and with proper English, I just have to blush," Sam replied with a giggle. Chasity was also giggling.

Sam only had a few days off after the wedding before having to return to work. They decided not to fly anywhere or even leave Maryland. They went and explored Maryland and Washington, D.C. They started off doing the tourist sites of Washington, D.C. Then they went to the Ocean City Boardwalk in Ocean City, Maryland. After playing on the boardwalk, shopping, and eating, they then found a little hotel nearby to stay the night. They went to Baltimore for Sam's last night of leave. They spent a romantic evening with dinner, dancing, and spending time in a somewhat pricey hotel. The hotel had all the amenities that they wanted. Sam had to go back to work the next morning, so he wanted a good night's sleep. This way he could awake refreshed and be ready to go for muster the next morning.

Sam had finally talked Chasity into returning to school for her nursing. So Chasity also had to get back so that she could get ready to start back to school. Between Sam's job with the Navy and Chasity returning to school, the two of them had little time together. Sam was on rotating shifts between day and evening. She started at Berkeley college in California. but with hearing about her mother's murder and going to the trial, she was just shy of completing her prerequisites for nursing school.

Now was her time to get those prerequisites completed so that she can move on to nursing school. She was actually going to follow her dream, and she would not have to do it alone. She would now have the support of her husband and best friend Sam Wilder.

Sam continued to learn more and more in his MOS (method of study) as time went on. He was actually starting to become more efficient with his MOS and actually moved up in rank. Chasity worked hard at her studies and was a very quick learner. She had always been a very intelligent person all through school. Unlike Sam who had to work hard to comprehend his studies.

Sam was an ordinary Joe. He liked simplicity in his life. He was not unintelligent by any means; he was just simple. Whereas Chasity was extraordinary. She had a good mind, good spirit, more complex thoughts, more complex taste in material needs, and wanted more out of her life and future.

* * * * *

A year had passed by since they were married, so they celebrated their first-year anniversary. Sam took her out to dinner and told her that he had something important to discuss with her. "Chasity, I love you with all my heart, and I know that you love me too. I believe that we should try to have a baby to complete our love and our family. How do you feel about that?" Sam said while waiting in anticipation.

"Well, Sam, you are full of surprises, are you not? To answer your question, I agree that having a baby with you would complete our family. I just want to know if you are going to be able to help out while I am in nursing school. I do not want to have to quit school again, and I really want my own career," Chasity replied in a matter-of-fact tone of voice.

Chasity was always very realistic about life matters, while Sam was more of a jump-in-first-and-we-will-figure-it-out-as-it-goes type of guy. "Chasity, I would not have mentioned it had I not been ready to take on the responsibility of taking care of the baby. We will work it out between the two of us. I will do everything in my power to take care of you and the baby," Sam replied with a smile. Sam always had a smile on his face even if he was nervous, as was this situation.

"Well, Sam, it looks like we are going to try to have a baby." Chasity smirked at Sam. Chasity would often hide her emotions behind her smirk.

* * * * *

After several months of trying to conceive, Chasity finally had some good news to tell Sam. Sam came home from work and went straight to the kitchen. He was often the cook and fixed the meals for himself and Chasity. Chasity would often stay after school to study with a study group.

Today was different; he saw Chasity in the kitchen waiting for him. "Are you all right, Chasity? Did you even go to school today? You never miss school. Are you sick?" Sam said in a concerned tone of voice.

"I am feeling a little morning sickness, Sam. But it should go away by the second or third trimester," Chasity said with a beaming smile.

It took Sam a moment to realize what she was saying. "Are you kidding me, or are you truly pregnant?" Sam replied. He then looked deeply into her eyes, and he could tell that she was not lying. Sam then started jumping around and shouting, "I am going to be a father! I am

going to be a father! You did it, my princess! You did it."
Sam and Chasity then embraced in a long, loving embrace,
knowing that they were going to be better parents than
their parents were.

Sam and Chasity did some calculations and figured
that Sam's four-year term of service to the Navy would
be up shortly after the baby was born. This meant that he
could apply to get his G.I. Bill to help them purchase a
house as well as help with other expenses, such as schooling
when the time would be appropriate.

Chasity had mentioned that he could always reenlist
and get the reenlistment bonus. In Sam's mind, this
was not an option. Sam was a good hard worker with a
spirit of gold. He loved working with his patients, and
his patients loved him. He would often get requested by
patients to be their corpsman.

Sam often did not work well with administration
or the officer in charge. This caused him to be busted in

rank due to insubordination a couple of times in his short time in the Navy. It seemed like as soon as he gained some rank, he would then have a write-up and be busted down again. He never did anything that warranted him to be released from the Navy with a Dishonorable Discharge, though. He just wanted to finish out his four years and return to civilian life with Chasity and their soon-to-be new baby.

Sam and Chasity were on cloud nine. They were approved for married housing and moved out of their little apartment. Chasity was doing well in school and was about to finish her semester of school. The pregnancy was going great. Chasity had picture-perfect ultrasounds that showed no complications. Sam was doing well and staying out of trouble, for now, and loved his job. They were making plans for after the Navy. They were going to move back to Florida.

Chasity was going to continue school, while Sam was going to get a job in the medical field. Everything was on track until Chasity got the letter in the mail followed up by a phone call.

"Chasity Leann Jones, your father, has been released from prison after an appeal and retrial. The judge determined time served and placed your father on parole." Chasity then just slumped over in her chair and started sobbing and cursing at the same time. Chasity then had it in her head as to what she had to do and what needed to be done. She was going to be the one to do it.

Chapter 12

Sam and Chasity Have a Baby

Another couple of years have passed, and Sam and Chasity are doing well.

Life was actually going better than well; it was going great for them. Sam is now out of the Navy with an Honorable Discharge. Sam was working as a cook in a fine-dining restaurant. He had a lot of restaurant experience prior to the Navy. He chose to go back to cooking while attending school. He was going to the university to be a schoolteacher. He opted for another career change in his life.

Chasity was getting ready to graduate nursing school with her ADN. They did end up buying a house in Pensacola, Florida, with the help of the G.I. Bill. Their son, Clint, was born without any complications and will be having his first birthday in a couple of months. Life was busy but very pleasurable for Sam and Chasity.

"Sam, can you help me with Clint? He is getting into everything, and I am trying to study for my finals," Chasity said in an exhausted voice.

"I can for a little while, but don't forget that I have a job to go to as well, as I must also study tonight," Sam said sarcastically. Even though they loved each other with all their heart and they loved their baby, life seemed to be getting a little tough at times. A different kind of tough than when they were teenagers. "Just think about it, Chasity. In four years from now, we will both have our degrees, and little Clint will be in kindergarten."

Sam was just starting his degree courses, while Chasity was finishing up hers. She had always wanted to be a nurse and help people that were in need. She got this attitude from wanting to be different from the way her mother and father were. As far as Sam knew, he never really knew what he wanted to do until the Navy changed him.

Working in the naval hospital, he would sometimes work in pediatrics. He fell in love with working with children. He also wanted this career since he was also one that struggled in school. Sam and Chasity thought that a nurse and a schoolteacher would make quite the power couple. A power couple that could provide for their child and be able to give him things that they didn't always have. "Sam, your child is getting into things again. Take him for a little while. I understand that you must also work and study, but my finals are very important to me," Chasity repeated to herself.

"Why is he my child when he is mischievous and getting into things, and he is your child when he is well-behaved?" Sam laughed while picking up the baby and going into the playroom.

Time had passed, and it was time for Sam to go to work. He was doing well as a cook, but the long days were getting to him. Between cooking at the restaurant, going to school, helping Chasity with the baby and the housework, trying to find time to study, Chasity doing her nursing school, and Chasity's studies, they found themselves starting to get on each other's nerves. They have had their moments in the relationship where this has happened before, but nothing was like this now.

Sam's charming smile, laughter, sarcasm, and wit was no longer charming but just annoying to her now. Chasity's cute little snoring, her cold feet, and her smirk, among other things, was also no longer cute to Sam. They made a decision a long time ago that two things would never happen. They would never argue, fight, or fuss at each other in front of their child or children. The other thing is that they would never go to bed mad at each other. If they should happen to go to bed mad at each other, then they would sleep on it and discuss it the next day. They both have held their word about this decision.

"So what do you think that we should do for Clint's first birthday? I think that we should have a nice celebration and invite all our friends and family over for a barbeque. You will do the cooking, and I will do the decorations and entertaining."

"Sounds like you have it all planned already. I would like it to be a little more intimate with not so many people, not so many decorations, and not so much entertaining. He is only turning a year old, and he will not remember this birthday anyway," Sam said in a grumpy voice. Sam was never one for big celebrations; he liked more little intimate ones.

"He may not remember his first birthday party, but we will. And I plan on taking plenty of pictures. This is just how it's going to be for my baby boy, and you should be proud for him," Chasity replied, not so happy with Sam.

It was time for the Birthday Party. Sam reluctantly helped with everything. He blew up Balloons, hung streamers everywhere. He even made a homemade cake with frosting. By the afternoon it seemed like the whole darn neighborhood showed up. Kids were screaming and running around. Adults were letting their kids run and get into mischief while they congregated and had conversation. Sam along with everything else was in charge of the games and food.. Chasity however was the social butterfly bragging on Clint. Clint made out like a bandit with all of the toys that he received in his presents. By the time that it was over there was cake, paper plates and red solo cups everywhere. After all the cleanup it was a long day for Sam and Chasity. Sam and Chasity were barely making it as a couple. They would put on their smiley faces in public, but both had mental health issues that were hiding in the shadows.

Chasity was recently diagnosed with bipolar and post-traumatic stress disorder. Sam was recently diagnosed with schizoid affective and bipolar disorder. This, along with the stressful life, was causing them to lean toward taking a break in their marriage. They thought about it and decided that it would be best if they tried to work it out for the benefit of the family. They did not want Clint to grow up with a single parent if they could help it.

"Sam, I need you to promise me that whatever happens, we will be friends and that you will take care of Clint," Chasity said with sadness in her face.

"I thought that we agreed to stay together and work it out for the sake of Clint," Sam replied, looking confused.

"We did. I am just saying if that scenario ever comes up that we cannot, then I want you to remember our friendship and take good care of our baby," Chasity replied with little to no expression.

"Chasity, I am tired of this back-and-forth. Of course, I will always remember our friendship. I love you with all that I am. I will also take care of our baby. I don't ever want this scenario to happen, though. Chasity, I know that look! Where are you going? What is on your mind? Come to bed and we can talk it out," Sam said with concern.

All Chasity would say was just, "Promise me." She was emotionless and just kept repeating "just promise me." Sam did the best that he could to comfort her while they went to bed for the night.

Chapter 13

Chasity Takes Revenge

Sam woke up the next morning, hoping that the talk that he had with Chasity had helped.

He noticed that she was not in the bed when he woke up. So he got up and opened the windows to let the sunshine in. He then went to see where Clint and Chasity were. He heard Clint crying in the living room. Chasity was nowhere to be found! He went and picked up Clint to soothe him and make his bottle and get him some food. Sometimes Chasity would go out jogging in the early morning before the heat came.

Sam was still a little worried, though, so he called Chasity's cell phone. He then heard her phone ring in the bedroom. He thought that was strange because she never leaves her cell phone. She also never leaves Clint alone for that matter. Sam called Chasity's friends to see if they had heard from her. There was no answer from some of them. The ones that did answer said that they had not heard from her in a while. Last time they had heard from her, she was depressed about how the marriage was going. They also said that she had continuing thoughts about her mother's death and her father being released on parole. She did not know how to handle her mental illness, so she was going to just leave everyone and be alone for a while. Sam thought that was very selfish of her to have these private thoughts and not involve him. In retrospect, it is all right to have private thoughts because he also has them. The only difference is that her thoughts affected the whole family.

It was too early to file a missing-persons report because it had not been twenty-four hours yet. That is one of the requirements in filing a missing-persons report. So he loaded the baby into the car and went for a drive along her jogging route. He did not see her. Then he went to some of her other favorite places that she liked to go to. He did not see her in those places. Last, he checked the local hospitals but did not find her there either.

Sam did everything that he could, but to no avail. Sam had to take off work and quit his schooling, because he had to take care of the baby and figure out where his wife had gone. Sam was in a very confused state of mind. The only thing that he could think about was that she had actually left them for good this time.

Chasity had always been one to leave at a moment's notice if something was on her mind and she needed to work something out. This time was different because she did not only leave Sam but she also left her baby. Sam just hoped and prayed that she would be all right and wouldn't hurt herself or others. He also was hoping that this time was like the time before when she would take a few days to clear her mind and come back home.

* * * * *

Days had passed, then weeks, and then a month. Sam was at his wit's end; he had to hire a babysitter for Clint so that he could go back to work. He hated to have to leave his thirteen-month-old with a babysitter, but he had to get back to work. While he was working and taking care of the baby, the case of his missing wife continued.

One month turned into three months, then six months. At this point, Sam took more time off work and packed the car so that he and his baby could go on a road trip to try and find Chasity. He had called his family back in Arkansas several times to see if they had heard anything that may be related to Chasity. They hadn't heard anything yet as far as Chasity's situation.

His aunt and uncle did say that Chasity's father was not around town anymore. They weren't sure if he left town and skipped probation or if he was just plain missing also. They said that Chasity's father's house had just recently been abandoned. This sparked curiosity in Sam as well as Sam's family.

Sam started thinking that Chasity could be tied to the disappearance of her father. If this was the case, then how were they tied together? Sam had no choice but to go back to Arkansas to try to figure out what was going on. Sam was in a hurry to get to Arkansas but had to make several stops to change and feed the baby. He also had to take bathroom breaks and get some food for himself.

Sam did not like fast food, and he was a vegetarian. So he would often stop at restaurants rather than fast food. This gave him an opportunity to get out of the car and take a little walk to stretch his legs. Their travels took them through the states of Mississippi, Alabama, Arkansas, and into Louisiana. Sam took some of the coastline, because Chasity loved the Coastline and visiting these Southern States. Sam did not stop in every city, but he stopped at the ones that Chasity loved best. Sam did get a hotel in Louisiana to get some rest and put the baby down for the night.

When he woke up, he automatically reached out for his wife to give her a morning hug and kiss to start the day, as he had done in the past. Even though it has been over six months since she has been missing, some habits are hard to break. He fed and put a fresh diaper on the baby prior to checking out of the hotel. It was going to be another long day.

* * * * *

After leaving the hotel in Louisiana, he circled back to Arkansas. He had not been back to Arkansas in Several years. He was glad that he was going to see his family, and that they would get a chance to see baby Clint. It was just sad that it had to be under these circumstances. Sam's uncle, aunt, and cousins took the baby in just as if it were one of their own. "Hey, Auntie, can you watch the baby while I go and talk with the sheriff?" Sam said while getting the baby bag ready.

"I sure can. I am just going to love this baby to bits," she said with a huge smile on her face.

"Thank you very much. It means a lot to me," Sam said as he rushed out the door. Sam headed over to the sheriff's office to see if they had heard anything or knew anything about the disappearance of either Chasity or her father. "Hello, Sheriff John, how are you today, sir?" Sam said.

The sheriff had his back turned to Sam and stated, "I am doing fine. I will be with you in a minute. Just have a seat right over there," he said while shuffling papers. When he turned and saw that it was Sam, he just smiled. "Well, I haven't seen you in a coon's age. How the heck are you doing, son?" he said as he laughed with his big belly shaking. Sam went on to explain the situation. All that the sheriff could say was that there were no leads on the whereabouts of Chasity's father. He also stated that he would be on the lookout if Chasity was in town. "Is there anything else that I can do for you, son?" he stated with a concerned look on his face.

"No, sir, just keep on the lookout, will you?" Sam replied in a frustrated tone.

"Will do, and you have a good day, you hear," the sheriff replied as he returned back to his paperwork.

When Sam returned home, he found that there were a lot more family and friends there. They had already started the cookout for Sam's return home. Everyone understood it was not a happy situation, but they wanted to see Sam and the baby. The cookout and music went on throughout the evening.

Sam stayed for four days prior to starting the trek home to Florida. Sam had a lot on his mind with the disappearance of Chasity, being a single parent to baby Clint, and wondering if he was going to stay in Florida or move back home to Arkansas.

He was on his way back to Florida when he got a call. It was Sheriff John. "Son, they just pulled a body out of the river. There was only one river that ran through town. The body was identified as Chasity's father. It appears that he was shot with a 12-gauge shotgun prior to being stuffed in a bag and thrown in the river. The bad thing about it is that we will have to eliminate suspects, including Chasity, whenever she is to be found. Do you understand the serious trouble Chasity could possibly be in? I just wanted you to hear it from the horse's mouth," the sheriff stated in a serious, matter-of-fact tone.

Sam thought about it long and hard. He didn't feel that she could do something like that, but Chasity has surprised him many times about things that she could do. He knew that her mental status was not the best, so maybe she pulled the trigger. Everyone knew how much she hated that man. It wasn't long after finding the body that a suspect had been taken in to talk to the sheriff.

According to the state police and sheriff's reports this is what the suspect said happened:

"Around the time of Chasity's disappearance in Florida was close to the time of death of her father. She, Chasity, returned to Arkansas and borrowed a 12-gauge shotgun from me. She called her father to see if she could come see him and catch up with him about her marriage and her son Clint. She truly had no intention of making small talk with her father. She went with the intention to kill him.

"When she went to her father's house, she knocked on the door. He opened the door and was as arrogant as ever. 'I just wanted to see you one last time and tell you that you are not my daughter. You never will be with that half-breed baby of yours.'

"When he started to speak again, she took the shotgun and shot him square in the chest. He died immediately. She and some of my friends that we knew from school put him in a bag and into the back of my pickup truck. We then went down and dropped him in the deepest part of the river. Afterward, we went back to the house and cleaned up the blood. We then took Chasity to the bus station, and she was never heard from again by anybody."

Chapter 14

Chasity Is Found

Sam said goodbye to his family, because he had to go back to Florida to tie up some loose ends.

He was still in Arkansas when the story came out in the local paper. He was saddened by the news, but he understood why Chasity did what she did. He just wished they would have been able to talk things out before it got carried away. Maybe she could have talked to her psychiatrist and therapist about this particular situation. He was even more sad that he had now lost a wife, and Clint had lost his mother.

Chasity will be on the run and knows enough to be able to survive for a long time without getting caught.

She could be anywhere at this moment in time. Sam is now officially on his own and a single father. He loves his baby boy, and he is willing to be the best father that he can for his child.

When he arrived back to Florida, the first thing that he did was go into the bedroom that he and Chasity had shared. He looked through all the memories that they had shared. The pictures, the souvenirs. He smelled her sweaters that she used to wear. He started to cry, but Clint beat him to it. It was time to feed and change the baby for the fourth time today. He had to stay strong for his child.

After he laid his baby down for the night, he went into the room and broke down crying. He was going to have to start his whole life over again. New job, new city, new surroundings, new friends, and new family.

Sam decided that he was not going to move back to Arkansas but return to Colorado. Then maybe onto California to see some family from his mom's side that he barely knew. First things first, he had to get out of Florida. He went back to the restaurant where he had been working and quit on the spot. The manager could tell the look on Sam's face and already knew what he was going to do. Sam was going to miss that restaurant because he was working his way up to being a chef.

Sam had some of his buddies from the restaurant in town, and his friend Chancellor from the Navy days, helped him pack the house out. Sam threw one last cookout before leaving Florida. None of Chasity's friends showed up even though they were invited. It was just Sam's friends giving him a final farewell.

The cookout went clear into the next morning, and some of his friends stayed the night. He got a good night's sleep, said goodbye to everybody, loaded baby Clint into the cab, and drove away. He drove away and never looked back. "Well, Clint, it looks like it is going to be you and me from now on. What do you think about hanging out with your good old dad full-time?" Sam said while glancing over at Clint. Clint just looked back at Sam and gave him a funny face as he passed gas. "Well, I guess that answers my question, does it not?" Sam said with a giggle. The first laugh that he had had in a long time. "We are going to get along just fine, little man. I made your mom a promise that I will take care of you, and I never break a promise," Sam said in his dad voice.

It only took a day and a half to get back to Arkansas, with a few stops that were made. When he got there, the family was as supportive as ever. Maybe even more now, considering the situation. "Hey, Auntie, how are you and Uncle doing today?" Sam said while holding a sleepy child.

"We are doing fine, Sam. How are you doing?" his auntie said with that big grin of hers. "The rest of the family is inside, waiting for you. How long will you be staying with us, Sam?" his auntie said, looking kind of sad because she already knew that he would be moving on.

"I guess that I can stay about a week, then I must be getting back on the road. I have decided that I will not be moving back to Colorado or stay here," Sam said with some contentment on his face. "I have decided to move back to California and look up my mama's side of the family," Sam said with some excitement in his voice.

Sam had grown up as an only child, being raised in Colorado. He was never able to be close with any family from either of his parents. He researched and found his aunts and uncles in California. He had also communicated with a few of his cousins. With Chasity missing and never to be heard from again, he wanted to get a fresh start. He not only wanted to get to know his mama's side of the family but he also wanted Clint to know his maternal grandma's side of the family. "Well, Auntie and Uncle, do you mind if I go ahead and eat something and go straight to bed? I must put little guy down, and I am exhausted myself."

"No problem, Sam. We'll talk in the morning and have plenty of time to visit this week," they both said.

* * * * *

The week had passed faster than expected. Everyone loved little Clint. Even the neighbors were invited to come by to see him. Sam said his goodbyes, not knowing when he would be coming back to Arkansas. He packed the few things that he had taken in, then he and Clint hit the road again. Sam stopped by Colorado along the way to show Clint where he was raised. Not that it made any difference to a one-year- old, but he also wanted to stop for himself. He went on through New Mexico and Arizona before reaching their destination in California.

Prior to leaving Florida, Sam went back to school and completed all of the requirements to be a Special Education teacher. He was able to get a hold of some of his Tias' and Tios' from his Mama's side and they put in a good word for him. So all he had to do was an interview and certain formalities, but the school had already promised him the position of Special education teacher. He also had a house to rent when he arrived in California.

As time went on, he had a chance to meet most of mama's side of the family. He also had a chance to meet some of his cousins. As usual, everybody fell in love with cute little baby Clint.

After being in California for a little over two years, he heard that he was going to get a promotion as the Director of Special Education of the school district that he was working in. He took the job, This afforded him to move out of his small home and into a bigger one.

As the years went on, he became established at the school district, and he decided that he was going to try to make tenure. He also returned to his martial arts practice and eventually became a third-dan black belt. Another change in his life was that he became a Buddhist. This was not shocking to people who really knew Sam. Sam always loved the Buddhist philosophy ever since he met a Buddhist in Navy boot camp.

Just as he was starting to settle in and get his life straight, he received the news that he had been waiting for many years. Chasity was found alive. She was living in New York. They found her at Penn Station acting very unusual. One could say that she was acting crazy. She got picked up on loitering charges as well as resisting arrest.

Chasity was silent and noncommunicative. When they ran her background, they were able to tie her to the murder of her father in Arkansas. When she went to trial the court room was full and she was the buzz of the town. People in the courtroom were saying how different she became from that sweet innocent girl in High School. How could she have done this? She came from a rich family and her parents gave her everything that she wanted. They remembered the case of her father killing her mother. Still most of the town stood by the father,not thinking that he was really that bad. That the murder was an accident. How could she dare kill the man that raised her. Even after she spoke out at her father's trail, nobody in town really took into consideration the depth of Darkness, Abuse, and Trauma that was in that house. This is why she could not let her father live after he was released on parole.

It was a short court case and trial due to Chasity's inability to speak on her own behalf. Her lawyer pleaded on her behalf. Her lawyer pleaded guilty by reason of insanity and battered women's syndrome. The Prosecutor had no objection, as long as she was put in a facility for life without parole. After hearing the case and taking a recess. The judge came back and addressed the court. She asked for the defendant to stand for sentencing. The judge said " As a woman I would not want to be in the position that you were in. No woman deserves to be treated the way that you were treated. Even worse, the trauma you suffered started as a child and the effects from this trauma affected your adulthood. That said, it is against the law for you to take vengeance and kill your abuser. So I am going to not place you in Prison, but you will spend the rest of your remaining life in a Criminal Mental Institution.

After the sentencing, Sam flew himself and Clint out to see Chasity on a couple of occasions. She was still noncommunicative but shunned away from them. She did not want to see them. All that she would do was hum and look out the window. She had dark piercing eyes, as if she was trying to look into the secrets of her life and what she could have done better. She also lost her smile altogether. Nobody ever saw her with a smirk or any implications of a smile anymore.

Sam took Clint back to California, never to return to Arkansas again. Sam had been keeping a journal of his and Chasity's relationship ever since they were teenagers in high school. Their first kiss, the Navy, Nursing School, the murder trials, her family history, his family history, the birth of Clint, etc. This journal will be given to Clint when he is old enough to understand the relationship of his father and mother.

About the Author

Dave Covington has an ex-wife and two stepsons.

He graduated from McClave High School in McClave, Colorado. He graduated in 1989. He served in the US Navy as a hospital corpsman toward the end of the Iraq War in 1991. He also served in the Army National Guard as a field medic. He served in units in Kansas and Wyoming.

After his military service, he went to Chadron State College. He attained a bachelor's degree in Special Education K-12. He taught in a self-contained classroom in Arkansas. He is retired but stayed involved in the Special Olympics.

He loves to travel around the world and the United States.

He is an active Buddhist monk.

www.ingramcontent.com/pod-product-compliance
Lightning Source LLC
Chambersburg PA
CBHW021112130626
46554CB00002B/647